#284

SUMMERS
AT LAMBSHEAD

John Burns

{ *A letter to the great-grandchildren*
of J.A. and Sally Reynolds Matthews }

{ In affectionate memory }

of

Sallie Reynolds *and* **John Alexander Matthews**,
at the time of the one hundredth anniversary of their marriage,
these personal reminiscences are recorded for their great grandchildren:

Susan Payne	Elizabeth Matthews Blanton
Sarah Payne	Laurence Matthews Lasater
Dale Lasater	Joseph Beck Matthews, II
Thomas Lindsay Blanton, III	Lane Lasater
Julia Matthews	Sally Matthews Blanton
Elizabeth Anne Blanton	Sally Ward Lasater
Marsha Densmore	William Watt Matthews
John McDougall Brittingham	Watt Matthews Casey, Jr.
Raymond Cloud Harrison, Jr.	Mary Blanton
Susan Alleyne Brittingham	Rebecca Trueheart Brown
Arthur Burns Densmore	Susan Reynolds Casey
Ardon Judd Harrison	Matthews Brown
Alan Lasater	Harold Hixon Brittingham, II
Rodney Lawrence Casey	John Brittingham Wallace
Anne Reynolds Wallace	John Alexander Matthews, IV
Brian Lasater	Frances Matthews Wallace
Margaret Clark Brittingham	Gerard Alexander Harrison
Ardon Berkeley Brown	Thomas Evans Brittingham, Jr.
John Clark Brittingham	Lucile Matthews Wallace
John Overton Brown	Kade Leggett Matthews
Sallie Reynolds Harrison	Penelope Brittingham
David Dutton Casey	Robert Scott Brittingham Wallace
Sally Mott Brittingham	Douglas Berkeley Harrison
Nancy Alston Judd	Sallie Matthews Judd

LAMBSHEAD is a word that has
been such an intimate part of my life that I seldom
stop to think what an unusual name it is for a West
Texas cattle ranch.

Many people, hearing it for the first time, assume that it
is a sheep operation; others, not unnaturally, conclude that the
head, or the skull, of a lamb had something to do with the
derivation of the name. Actually, it was originally taken from
that of the creek that bends around the headquarters of the
ranch, runs beneath a limestone bluff in front of the house, and
flows on through the old Culver pasture and that part of the
ranch known as "the valley," to empty into the Clear Fork of the
Brazos River. The creek, in turn, took its name from Thomas
Lambshead, an early settler who arrived in the area in the mid-
1850s.

Little is known of Mr. Lambshead, but Roscoe
Conkling, in *The Butterfield Stage*, identifies him as a farmer and
the manager of a relay station for the Butterfield Overland Mail,
which was located near the mouth of Lambshead Creek, on the
site of which there is now a commemorative marker. A friend
and neighbor of Lambshead was Jesse Stem, the federal agent for

a small tribe of Comanches, who for a few years lived on a reservation that included a portion of what is now the northwest part of the ranch. Confining Comanches to a reservation in this area was not a success (nor in any other area for that matter) and the effort was abandoned. Jesse Stem was killed by Indians – Kickapoos rather than Comanches – and, as recounted in *Interwoven*, his widow and children returned to Ohio to live. Lambshead's name is attached to an original survey located a few miles west of the relay station he operated, but there is no known record of what eventually became of him.

Also a neighbor of Lambshead and Stem was Lt. Colonel Robert E. Lee who, for some two years was stationed at Camp Cooper, located in what is now the Tecumseh pasture of the ranch. In a letter to his wife, Lee described the place as a "desert of dullness. There was not, in truth, nearly as much activity during the pre-Civil War years as during the war itself and in the late 1860s, when Comanche and Kiowa raids terrorized the area and brought about the establishment of Fort Griffin, several miles down the river from Camp Cooper. Lambshead Ranch has a rich historical heritage, and what some writers have called "the cutting edge of the frontier" passed through it. When Newton C. Givens built what is known as "the old Stone Ranch" in 1856, a traveler did not find beyond it another permanent dwelling until he reached El Paso. Comanches had a way of inhibiting settlement.

However it became attached to the area, the name Lambshead has, throughout this century, been one of fond association to the family of Sallie and John Matthews. As the chart in the back of this booklet shows, it was a large family and it has increased steadily through the years. They had nine children and twenty grandchildren, among the latter of whom one of the parents of each of you is numbered.

In *Interwoven*, a book with which you are all, of course, intimately familiar and which is now a classic, Sallie Matthews describes her life as a girl on the outer edge of the northwest frontier of Texas, her marriage to John Matthews in 1876, the births of their nine children and the details of their lives until 1900, in a number of locations, nearly all of which were within a short radius of what came to be their permanent ranch headquarters at Lambshead. The last line of *Interwoven* is, "So the closing year of the century was marked for us by the birth of our last child and the marriage of our eldest."

The marriage was that of their daughter, Mary Louise, always known as May, to Thomas L. Blanton. The young newlyweds occupied a house next door to the Matthews family in Albany. It is easy to understand how Thomas L. Blanton, Jr., born in 1900, could conceive of the idea that he had two homes, two mothers, two fathers, and attach the words "Othermama" and "Otherpapa" to his grandparents. And it was inevitable that the same address should be adopted by his siblings and, subsequently, by the fifteen other grandchildren of Sallie and John Matthews. I have occasionally thought that these terms might sound a bit "cute" to persons hearing them for the first time, but to the Matthews grandchildren they were, and are, as natural as Mother and Dad, and in these pages that is the way I shall refer to them.

1897 MARKED the first appearance of a cattle camp on the site of the present Lambshead headquarters. In 1906, this was enlarged to become the residence of the Matthews family (although they also spent several years during that decade in Austin and Fort Worth), and it was home to Othermama and Otherpapa until their move back to Albany in 1929.

It continued to seem like home to their children as well after the latter's marriages and establishment of homes of their own. Like young Tom Blanton, the grandchildren, especially the older ones, though not residing just next door to their grandparents, grew up looking on Lambshead as another home. None of them can remember the time he or she first went to Lambshead; most of them were carried there as infants. And each was there often enough not to be able to remember when Lambshead first became a part of his or her awareness. It has always been there. It has been there as an amalgam of sights, of sounds, of fragrances (and odors), of tastes and of experiences that attach uniquely to this one spot and that combine to create the special consciousness that will always be evoked by the word Lambshead.

FAR BEYOND the sensory perceptions, it was the characters and the personalities of Othermama and Otherpapa that shaped the Lambshead experience and made of it the lasting memory and influence it has been for all of us. From the time they went there to live, it was an established custom for their children and grandchildren to make extended visits and for the grandchildren, in fact, to be left for periods with their "other parents." They must have been the champion baby sitters of all time. Not that there was ever very much sitting around Lambshead; five of the seven eldest grandchildren were boys, and Otherpapa used to refer to them as "cheap labor." Othermama was equally interested in seeing that her granddaughters were productively occupied without ever making life at Lambshead seem in any way onerous.

Othermama's character emerges as clearly as an etching from her own words in *Interwoven*, even though she did not purposely intend to paint a self-portrait when she wrote her reminiscences. But Otherpapa, while naturally figuring prominently in *Interwoven*, is not distinguishable in the very special colors that enlivened his personality and which, through endless recountings by those who knew him, have come to lend a sense of legend to his person. So if in these pages he receives "star billing," it does not mean that summers at Lambshead were shaped or dominated more by him than by Othermama; it just seemed so at the time.

The exterior of the main house at Lambshead has always looked to me very much as it does now, and the inside, while modified on several occasions through the years, also has the same appearance and feel, although it was never again quite the same after Othermama and Otherpapa moved their residence back to Albany. We have a hard time today recalling, or figuring out, where everyone slept when there was a big crowd on hand, and in my memory, there were few times when there was not at least a fair sized one. In the very early days, what is now the library was a bedroom (with a wash basin in the corner where the telephone is now, with faucets that ran water in a stream about the size of a cigarette); there were three other bedrooms, including Othermama's and Otherpapa's. Cot-like beds were strung along the front porch, and with the remodeling that turned the front bedroom into a library, window seats were constructed on both sides of the fireplaces in that room and the living room that could accommodate children not yet five feet tall, of whom there were always several. However everyone slept, everyone was always comfortable and there was always room for another. The boys slept at the cowboys' bunkhouse, known at Lambshead as "the shack," and to graduate to that level of dormitory distinction was looked on as something of a Lambshead "bar mitzvah" by a Matthews grandson.

Meals were cooked and served in the main ranch house until 1923 when the first "cook shack," as the separate kitchen/dining room is called, was constructed. Everyone – family, guests, cowboys and passing strangers – ate together, then as now; there was always a plate and a place at the table for one more. All the "regulars" had assigned places, marked by napkin rings, Otherpapa's being easily the largest and most elaborate in design. Plates were enamel and I can still recall being sent away from the table, along with Sallie Joe Casey, for laughing at the noise one of the cowboys made as he cut up cabbage with his knife and fork. Children were expected to adhere to recognized standards of comportment at the dining table as elsewhere, and dismissing grandchildren from the table was not unusual with Otherpapa. I doubt if there is one of the elder group of us who at one time or other did not experience this manifestation of grandparental disapproval.

It was not because of laughter itself that Sallie Joe and I were sent from the table. Meals at Lambshead, and later in Albany, and in fact wherever Othermama and Otherpapa presided at table, were always sociable, jolly occasions with never-lagging conversation, interspersed with much laughter. We were dismissed because Otherpapa knew we were laughing at the cowboy and he did not want him embarrassed.

Otherpapa was interested in food and the Lambshead table was a bountiful and excellent one. Beef, of course, was a staple and in the autumns, numbers of hogs, both domestic and wild, were killed. The latter were actually domestic hogs (and their progeny) that had been turned loose to shift for themselves, which they did very well on the pecans and other mast found along the river. In only a short time, they would revert to wild characteristics, grow tusks and acquire the wild flavor that markedly distinguishes them. The most memorable pork product of Lambshead was the sausage that Otherpapa mixed with his own special blend of peppers and chili powder, the ingredients being supplied by a Fort Worth establishment with which he corresponded regularly. I don't know what its real name was, but Otherpapa's orders, addressed simply to "The pepper store east of the Courthouse," Fort Worth, never failed to be filled promptly, and the product was the spiciest, tangiest sausage I have ever eaten. I have not found its equal since.

There were always several dairy cows, Holstein and

Jersey, which provided gallons of milk daily. The grandchildren frequently tried to help, getting in the way more than anything else. The milk was turned over to Othermama, who kept it in stone jars on metal shelves draped with wet cloths. It would not be possible for anyone to be more meticulous with anything than Othermama was with the milk at Lambshead, and she devoted a lot of time to its care, rarely entrusting it to anyone working in the kitchen. She supervised the making of the butter, and I remember doing a good deal of churning, a job I rather liked as it was interesting to see the big clots of butter forming in the milk. There was always clabber on hand, an item of which Otherpapa was extremely fond. The very earliest single incident in my memory with which Otherpapa is associated was when, holding out a large spoonful of clabber, he asked me if I would like some ice cream. That was my first taste of clabber and I have never learned to like it; probably I wouldn't have anyway, but I sure didn't after that. Otherpapa enjoyed practical jokes, and I was always an inviting target, as might be deduced from the clabber encounter.

HOMINY was another favorite dish of Otherpapa's, and he once asked Othermama to have it every day until he signaled a stop. I don't know how long this endurance contest lasted, but Otherpapa had great staying power. Once when Othermama was a patient in Nix Hospital in San Antonio, Otherpapa purchased a wholesale quantity of hominy, which he distributed to everyone on Othermama's floor, patients and staff alike.

Otherpapa was a good cook, and he always asked each prospective cowboy if he could cook. It was his belief, frequently expressed, that any man on a ranch should be able to prepare his own food if necessary. He once asked Joe Blanton if he could cook and, on receiving an affirmative answer, inquired further: "Can you make bread?" "No," replied Joe. "Then you can't cook," continued Otherpapa.

He was the autocrat of the table, whatever and wherever the meal, and was nearly always in control of any discussion. Firm in his own opinions and convictions, he was tolerant and respectful of the views of others. No matter how sharply he might disagree with them or how categorical the differences, he could argue dispassionately. As I have mentioned before, one never knew who, or how many, might be on hand when meals were announced (it is still the same at Lambshead), and this always added variety and interest to the dining table, which was, as I am sure you have concluded, an important focal point of family exchange. One day, among the guests was a man who held, and began to voice, anti-Jewish sentiments, oblivious that one of the other guests was himself Jewish. Suddenly aware that most of those present were staring rather fixedly at their plates, he divined the reason and halted abruptly in mid-sentence. A heavy, awkward silence descended on the table, but not for long. Leaning toward the speaker, Otherpapa counseled, in a stage whisper, "Just go on as if nothing had happened." This advice reflected no prejudice; it was just Otherpapa's way of handling an embarrassing situation, which, like all situations, he preferred to meet "head on." I cannot recall ever hearing Otherpapa say anything that reflected prejudice toward any person's race, religion or politics. The saying that in the old West a man was accepted as a gentleman until he proved himself otherwise found its embodiment in Otherpapa.

I HAVE IMPLIED that there was a good deal of work at Lambshead, and there was, but there was a lot of play as well. Each grandchild, at an early age, was taught by Otherpapa to ride and by Othermama to swim, and both were able instructors.

Those were the happy days when the Clear Fork of the Brazos really was clear and not carrying a heavy load of Abilene sewage. There were wonderful swimming and fishing holes throughout the length of its course across the ranch as well as sunny, rippling shoals, pleasant for picnicking and gathering mussel shells.

The favorite swimming hole at the time that Othermama was teaching me to swim was at Buzzard's Peak, which was a popular camping ground those days. We also swam and picnicked at the William Reynolds Crossing, the Davis Crossing, the mouth of Cottonwood and Burkett Bend. Most of these are still favored camping areas, although, as I have indicated, the river is not the great recreational benefit it was in those days. Othermama had been taught to swim in the Clear Fork by Tonkawa Indian squaws, and I imagine she used the same methods in teaching her grandchildren. All of them developed into competent swimmers, and there was never any concern on the part of the parents or grandparents about children being around the river from the age of six on.

Camping on the Clear Fork was a regular summer treat. At least it was a treat for most of the participants; not all of Otherpapa's daughters and granddaughters have been outdoors enthusiasts. One who wasn't was my mother, but she would put in an appearance for brief periods anyway. One story that stayed with Mother all of her life dated back to a time in her late teens when, at a hot July noontime dinner at a camp on the river, Otherpapa served her plate with a generous quantity of beef and beans, which she contemplated briefly and then rejected with some emphasis. "Well, just what would you like to have to eat?" inquired Otherpapa with more than a touch of sarcasm. "Orange ice and chocolate cake," responded Mother decisively, thereby triggering a reaction only slightly less explosive than that which greeted Oliver Twist when he asked for a second helping of porridge. Mother said she was also lightly scolded by Othermama for making an issue of the subject instead of just taking the beef and beans to the garbage pail. Like her father,

Mother often approached things "head on." Incidentally, orange ice and chocolate cake remained her favorite dessert all her life.

Otherpapa was a conscientious instructor of riding, as was and is his son, Watt, and while some of the grandchildren "sat a horse" better than others, they all rode well and knew the basic rules of approaching and handling a horse. In those days the small saddles that belonged to J. A., Jr., and Watt as boys were used in turn by each of the grandchildren, and they must have been put atop old Indian, Chappo, Alec, Shorty, Bobby and the other "kid horses" literally thousands of times before they were retired to the back porch of Lambshead house, where they now sit atop wooden "horses," treasured mementos. Otherpapa was a fairly stern instructor and rarely countenanced frivolity among his charges. Loping was seldom allowed and I can recall only a few times when Otherpapa permitted a "race" among the grandchildren. His regular mount was a bay named Dodson, one of the roughest gaited horses I have ever been aboard, and he set the pace to which all his entourage was expected to adjust. By the time the younger – Brittingham and Judd – grandchildren came along, Watt had become the principal tutor and he was an equally outstanding one.

AUNT ETHEL Casey was an ardent and excellent horsewoman and always generous in shepherding a crowd of "rannyhan" (Watt's collective name for his younger nieces and nephews) riders.

She was a bright figure, with her English saddle and riding clothes, on Smoky, a sharp little grulla that was her favorite mount for a number of years. Riding with Aunt Ethel was more fun than riding with Otherpapa, as we would often take swimming suits, and perhaps a picnic lunch, for a trip to the river. Otherpapa was more likely to want to ride among the cattle and certainly not to go swimming. The Overton place, where we were always certain to have a tasty handout from Miss Alice, and the Putnam Ranch at Camp Cooper were among other favored objectives when Aunt Ethel was doing the navigating. And when the wild plums were ripening, we would take sacks and gather quantities from thickets scattered across the ranch. Wild plums make one of the finest of all jellies.

All the horses at Lambshead during those years were geldings, and it was Otherpapa's theory that it was cheaper to buy mature mounts than to cope with breeding, foaling and breaking horses on the ranch, however much the cowboys would have enjoyed the latter activity. I can recall only once, in fact, during my summers at Lambshead, when there were any "broncs" around, and they were only semi-broncs that Otherpapa had purchased from the neighboring Cook Ranch. I remember them well – there were seven: two bays, Streak and Snip; two roans, Leonard (one of Gene Pickard's string) and Campfire; two duns, Maverick and Dude (named for Mrs. W. I. Cook, whose nickname it was); and a sort of dun-white paint, a glamorous looking horse with a "glass" eye, named Sheik. These horses were not really bucking broncos, and it was my dearest wish to ride one, a wish never realized as far as I can remember, that or any other year.

I recall another occasion when Otherpapa bought a horse that had been represented to him as being well broken and tractable. The first morning that he was brought in with the rest of the horses he repeatedly refused to enter the corral and, once inside as the result of the combined efforts of several cowboys, he pawed at the one trying to bridle him, bit other horses and caused a commotion in general. This went on for two or three mornings with the same performance repeated daily. About the fourth day, after the cowboys and other riders had departed, and the horses had been turned out into the horse pasture, Otherpapa took a rifle and summoned Jim Reynolds to drive him, in the Model T Ford, out into the pasture where, after a short search, he found the horse for which he had paid a substantial sum only a few days before, raised the rifle and put a bullet neatly through his head. "Drive on," said Otherpapa to Jim. At least that is the way Jim immediately recounted the episode to me. I was curious why Jim, rather than I, had been pressed into duty, as I was Otherpapa's regular summer driver. I imagine that he suspected that I might not be of the kidney for that particular undertaking. If so, he was probably right; killing animals has never ranked high on my scale of enjoyment.

OTHERPAPA made sure his grandsons respected guns and handled them carefully. I can recall several times being assigned to the back seat of the Model T with a twelve gauge shot gun and firing at jack rabbits, crows atop fence posts and various other targets that Otherpapa would select, the recoil of the gun jarring me back to the middle of the seat. "Drive on," Otherpapa would say, without comment on the quality of the marksmanship.

The summary dispatch of the untrainable horse was typical of Otherpapa. While he had every reason to return him to the man from whom he had made the purchase, and demand a refund of his money, he knew that the horse would be resold and that eventually what he himself did would have to be undertaken by someone else, with considerable damage being done by the horse in the meantime. He would not resell the horse himself, or even make a gift of him, as he was not only worthless to any ranch string, but a clear and serious liability. At the time, I thought the action cold-blooded; later I saw it was the honest and, on the whole, kind thing to do. Otherpapa was always solicitous of the welfare of all his animals.

The fact that there were almost no serious injuries or accidents during the countless hours that were devoted to riding at Lambshead can probably be attributed to the care that Otherpapa devoted to the training of his grandchildren in the handling of horses. A white Welsh pony named Jumbo shied out

Lambshead in Winter, c. 1915

Lambshead in Summer, c. 1919

Cowboys leaving for the day's work.

Anne Blanton on Chappo, Bill Blanton on Sandy, Susanne Burns on Jumbo
(the morning Susie broke her arm)

L to R: Susette Matthews Burns, Otherpapa (holding Sallie John Casey), Susanne Burns, May Matthews Blanton, Anne Blanton, Othermama.

Othermama and Otherpapa with grandchildren. Latter, L to R, standing: Tom Blanton, Jr., Matt Blanton, Sallie Joe Casey (held by Otherpapa) seated: Susanne Burns, Joe Blanton, Bill Blanton, John Burns, Anne Blanton.

Watt and Joe Matthews.

Sallie and Lucile Matthews.

Lucile Matthews and John Burns

Otherpapa and granddaughters, L to R, Susanne Burns, Anne Blanton, Sallie Joe Casey, Mary Casey

Grandchildren, L to R, Sallie Joe Casey, Betty Burns, Watt Casey, John Matthews, Mary Casey, Bill Blanton, John Burns

Camping at the River

The first cook shack

Sallie Joe Casey

Tom Brittingham has an early riding lesson

Christmas 1926 at Lambshead. L to R, Mary Casey, John Burns, Otherpapa, Betty Burns, Sallie Joe Casey, Watt Casey.

Morning riders: John Burns, Sallie Joe Casey, John Matthews, Mary Casey.

One of the last pictures of Otherpapa - with Susan Judd.

from under my sister, Susanne, who suffered a broken arm as a result, but with that one exception, none of the Matthews grandchildren sustained any injury worth remarking from a riding accident as a child. The same remarkable record has been continued by the great-grandchildren, carefully schooled by their Uncle Watt. Not that there have not been many separations of riders from horses at Lambshead; that is to be expected whenever horses and people come together on a steady basis. But persons taught to be alert, not to take horses for granted, and how to disengage safely when the occasion demands, are less likely to be hurt than casual or over-confident riders. Perhaps luck has been an element in all this, but luck has had a powerful assist through the years at Lambshead.

As I have mentioned, I was Otherpapa's regular driver whenever I was at Lambshead. This job had a sporty element to it, as he basically expected a car to go anywhere a horse could go. He was continually directing me to leave the road and take off across the pasture for any of a variety of reasons, usually to look at cattle. We got stuck quite a lot and had frequent flat tires, but the wonder to me, in retrospect, is that we were not constantly immobile for one reason or another. This is where I learned to drive and no one ever gave me a lesson. I "fell into" my job more or less by accident. One afternoon of the summer of 1925, Otherpapa decided that he wanted to make a trip to Hay Ford, one of the sub-headquarters on the ranch, and could find no one around to drive for him. But I was there, aged eleven, and transported with delight to have him inquire, seriously, if I knew how to drive a car. I responded with an immediate, enthusiastic and altogether unjustifiably self-confident, "Sure," even though Otherpapa was well aware that my driving experience had been limited to the few times when I had been permitted to bring the Model T from its shed to the front of Lambshead house. "All right, we'll go to Hay Ford," said Otherpapa and off we lurched, much to his amusement. We managed to make the round trip of some twelve miles with no lasting damage to either the car or to any animals along the way, and from that day, I was his regular driver whenever I was at Lambshead. This involved a year or two with the Model T, then one with a Model A touring car, and finally a few with a small Buick sedan of which Otherpapa was particularly fond and which was an exceptionally good car.

Otherpapa, as I have already indicated, was "work oriented," and he made full use of the presence of his "cheap labor" grandsons in a wide variety of projects, such as concreting the floors of barns (with the concrete mixed by hand), surveying, cleaning out septic tanks, building fences and cattle guards, and repairing roads, an ever necessary chore. My assignment as driver carried the unfortunate double jeopardy of having me right there in plenty of time for concrete mixing, post hole digging, septic tank cleaning, etc., but of disqualifying me for horse riding activity unless Otherpapa himself was going to ride, which by that time was becoming increasingly rare.

HE WAS UP before five, and anyone awake at the time could see him, with his flashlight, making the rounds of the headquarters buildings, checking I don't know what. The boys of the family were expected to be up with the sun, and this expectation never failed to be realized, thanks to a bell mounted on two poles just behind the cook shack that was rung soon after daylight, the clangor of which was enough to awaken a sound sleeper half a mile away. Since it was not more than twenty feet from the sleeping porch of the bunkhouse, its effect was electric. I would recognize its clarion peal anywhere in the world.

The grandsons usually took turns wrangling the horses, and this required a dawn round of the horse pasture to be sure that a sufficient number of mounts were on hand for the cowboys by the time the latter finished breakfast. I grew to hate this assignment, not because it required me to roll out an hour earlier than usual, or because I didn't enjoy riding in the earliest light of day, but because I was so poor at it. It didn't matter in which direction I would start out, the horses were always grazing in another. I became convinced that they moved around behind me as I circled the pasture with a mounting feeling of semi-panic, ever more conscious of the sun rising above the horizon and picturing all too graphically the scene of the group waiting at the Lambshead corral. Sometimes when I would arrive, driving a pitifully small herd, I would find that a number of other horses had wandered in voluntarily. Only once did I finally give up and ride back empty-handed, turning the "night horse" over to one of the cowboys who shortly had the corral filled. The memory of that humiliation is still vivid. I occasionally wondered later if my performance as a horse wrangler had anything to do with Otherpapa's selection of me as his driver.

Even to this day, there is no sound that is more pleasing to me than rain on a roof, but none has ever been quite comparable to that on the roof of the Lambshead bunkhouse. This meant not only that there would be no work that day (assuming it was more than a passing shower), but also that everyone would be in the best of spirits. I do not mean to imply that there was ever any evidence of gloom or unhappiness at Lambshead; quite the contrary. But with rain the scarce commodity it has always been in West Texas, and as vital as it is to ranching, a "gully washer" generated an aura of good feeling all around. The morning would be spent telephoning neighboring ranches (or receiving calls from them), always with the opening inquiry of "How much have you had?" (This ritual has not changed an iota through the years.) Then, when the rain had stopped, Otherpapa and I would set out for the farm, Hay Ford and other work centers of the ranch to check the rain gauges, doing a fair amount of slipping and sliding in the process.

During the 1920s, Otherpapa was thinking of the possibility of someday dividing Lambshead among his children and, although he ultimately discarded this idea, he devoted a lot of time and effort to a projection of the most equitable possible partition. He devoted a lot of his grandsons' time and efforts as well, and it was a dismal forecast to hear Otherpapa ask Watt to "call Ben (Uncle Bennie Reynolds, Othermama's brother who lived in Throckmorton) and see if he can come out next week and bring his transit." This meant a period of some of the most cordially disliked work that the grandsons were called on to undertake. I always secretly hoped that Uncle Bennie might turn out to have a sprained ankle or some other disability that would prevent his appearance. He never did, and would arrive punctually with his daughter, Ivy, at the wheel of his car. We chopped sight lines and located land corners and "bearing trees" all over the ranch, and Bill and Joe Blanton, Jim Reynolds and I dragged surveyor's chains many a mile, shouting "stick" and "stuck" as we tramped through prickly pear and mesquite brush, uphill and downhill and across every sort of botanical and geological feature the ranch offers, clutching metal pins with pieces of red rag tied in the loop at the top to mark our course. Uncle Bennie was, as the saying goes, a "character," and besides being a surveyor and cattleman was also an attorney, serving as County Attorney of Throckmorton County for many years. Perhaps the salient point in my memory of him was his ability to smoke a cigarette until it literally disappeared under his Mark Twain style moustache, which I kept expecting to burst into flame, but which never did.

One element for which we were grateful was that we would nearly always stop work in time for Otherpapa and Uncle Bennie to have a game of dominoes or forty-two back at Lambshead before supper. Otherpapa was very fond of dominoes, and, sometimes, if no better prospects were around, he would even summon some of his grandchildren to the table. I was not very good at this game, and have been told often that I would sit for some time in deep contemplation of my hand, leading others to assume I was trying to find a way to make twenty rather than fifteen, before finally sighing, "Pass."

There was always a lot of card playing at Lambshead, and it was not unusual for as many as six or eight of the grandchildren and friends to spread out multiple hands of solitaire on the floor of the library, a spirited competition that took a rapid toll of the cards. Othermama taught me to play chess, but I don't remember ever beating her, or anyone else for that matter.

OTHERPAPA was on the move a lot, and even when he wasn't, he wanted me within earshot so that we could be off with no delay should the notion strike him.

Consequently, I was with him a great deal of the time and came to know him intimately. My memory of him, even though he has been gone thirty-five years, is indelible, and I can picture him and hear his voice as clearly as though I had said goodbye to him yesterday. Curiously, despite the span of years during which I knew him so well, my memory of him is exactly the same; he never seemed to me to change. He was not tall, but he was solidly built and gave the impression of being larger than he actually was; at least he gave me that impression. He walked with a purposeful and determined gait, and I have no single recollection of ever seeing him run. And certainly not stroll. He rode a horse exactly the same way, at a steady, hard trot, and he wanted his grandchildren neither loping ahead nor lagging behind.

He was, I believe, the most predictable individual I have ever known. He practiced industry, honesty, straightforwardness (sometimes brutal frankness), and he was intolerant of shortcomings in these characteristics in others. Once, driving to Fort Worth, Otherpapa had the car stop to ask a man walking along the road where he was going. (He was continually stopping to converse with people along the road, sometimes hailing down total strangers in other automobiles for this purpose.) When the man said he was going to Mineral Wells, he was invited to ride. In the ensuing conversation, he naturally learned that the car was going to Fort Worth. On arrival at Mineral Wells, he said, "I think I'll just ride on in to Fort Worth with you." "No, you won't," rejoined Otherpapa. "If you had said you were going to Fort Worth, it would be different, but you said you were going to Mineral Wells and you're getting out at Mineral Wells." He got out.

OTHERPAPA not only believed in – and practiced – telling nothing but the truth, he also preferred hearing, and telling, the whole truth. Everyone always knew exactly where he stood with Otherpapa and exactly where Otherpapa stood on any issue, no matter how sensitive or controversial; similarly, he wanted straight answers to his own questions. He used to counsel his children and grandchildren that they would never learn anything if they didn't ask questions, and certainly he set them a good example. Persons to whom he had just been introduced, including ladies, were quite as likely as not to be asked their age. I recall an occasion one summer when Uncle "Pat" Casey arrived for a visit of a day or two – as was customary with the Matthews sons-in-law whose families were spending the summer at Lambshead – bringing with him a business friend, probably from San Antonio. After introductions and a minimum of pleasantries, the conversation was off to a meaty start, with Otherpapa turning to the visitor and inquiring: "What is your approximate annual income?" On encountering friends he might not have seen for some time, it was by no means unusual for Otherpapa to follow the standard greeting of "How have you been getting along?" with "Financially, I mean." A curious thing about all this was that people not only took no offense, but almost always would respond fairly specifically. One who failed to do so on one occasion, to his subsequent costly amusement, was Tom Byrne. Tom's sister, Grace, was married to Watt Reynolds, and Tom could not have been a more beloved member of the family had he been born into it. He was a man of great charm, handsome, and always extremely well dressed. On one visit to Lambshead, he appeared in an especially fine pair of slacks for which he had paid a price that today would be comparable to, say, $60. Otherpapa, who was not, as a matter of fact, much given to commenting on people's clothing so long as it was not markedly different from everyone else's, was moved to compliment Tom on his slacks, and, predictably, to follow up by asking what they had cost. Tom, confronted with the unexpected dilemma of telling the truth and suffering a possible, even likely, derisive rejoinder, or trying what we would term a "white lie," opted for the latter and replied as casually as possible: "I think they cost about twenty dollars, Uncle John," hoping therewith to have closed that particular subject of conversation. He hadn't. "Order me two pair from wherever you got yours," instructed Otherpapa.

Otherpapa not only expected straight answers to his own questions, he provided direct ones to queries addressed to him, sometimes to the point of what might be termed unnecessary candor. One day in front of the bank in Albany, he encountered a lady whose husband had simply disappeared a week or ten days previously and whose absence had prompted a certain amount of conjecture around Albany. Coming straight to the point in greeting her, Otherpapa asked if she had heard anything from her husband, whom we might call Frank. The lady responded that she had not, but that she was just preparing to leave for Abilene to look at a corpse in the morgue that had not been identified. "Do you think it might be Frank, Judge Matthews?" the lady asked plaintively. "No," replied Otherpapa with decision, "it won't be Frank." "Well, don't you think Frank's dead?" continued the lady. "No, Frank's not dead," volunteered Otherpapa. "He's just changed his range." And, as it developed, he had.

Another recipient of unsolicited information was Oscar Calloway, whose name during those years appeared regularly on the ballot in the Democratic primary elections. Once or twice he ran against Uncle Lynn (Thomas L.) Blanton, who for some twenty years represented the seventeenth district of Texas in Congress. When Uncle Lynn announced in 1928 that he would seek the Senate seat then held by Earle B. Mayfield, a large field of aspirants emerged as candidates to succeed him in the House of Representatives, among them, yet again, Oscar Calloway. The campaign was a heated one and all the family were naturally interested; not only in Uncle Lynn's race (he lost, this being the election that sent Tom Connally, eventually chairman of the Foreign Relations Committee, to the Senate), but also in who would take his seat in the House. One day in Albany, Mr. Calloway came up to Otherpapa and said, "Judge Matthews, I know that Judge Blanton is your son-in-law, so naturally I've never asked you to vote for me in my past races for Congress. But with Judge Blanton running for the Senate this year, I want to request your support." "Well, Mr. Calloway," replied Otherpapa, "I live in Throckmorton County and that's in the fifteenth district so I can't vote in your race." "But," he added firmly, "if I did live here I'd vote for R. Q. Lee." This gratuitous intelligence seemed not to discourage Mr. Calloway, and he and Otherpapa discussed the qualities of Mr. Lee at some length. Mr. Calloway maintained that he was too old, a contention of doubtful political appeal to someone several years older than either of them. Lee, a Cisco cattleman, was elected but died not long after taking his seat; in a special election, Uncle Lynn returned to Congress.

OTHERPAPA took an active interest in politics, and during the summers that I drove for him, we attended many campaign gatherings when one or more candidates would appear. He never failed to vote, and customarily let everyone know exactly how he was going to vote, be the election one involving individuals or issues such as the repeal of the 18th (prohibition) amendment. The latter was a hotly debated question, and wherever we went that summer – which, as usual, was many places – Otherpapa let it be known, unequivocally, that he favored repeal. I knew his presentation by heart. It began with, "Now I am not a drinking man myself ..." (which he wasn't; had he been, he would have said so) and continued through a series of examples of his assessment of the failure of prohibition, ending with the judicious observation that there was no use trying any longer.

Othermama, who probably recognized that prohibition up until that time had, in fact, failed, still hoped that it might succeed and was unswayed by Otherpapa's arguments. She never countered with any of her own, but I am sure that Otherpapa harbored no illusions that he was making any conversions under his own roof. On one occasion that heated summer, when the family occupied their customary pew in the Matthews Memorial Church, Reverend J. A. Owen, the pastor for many years, began his sermon on an announced text, but gradually departed from the main theme thereof to consider whiskey, prohibition and the coming election. Warming to the subject, he urged his flock to go to the polls and retain the ban against spirits in Texas. After some minutes of this exhortation, Otherpapa rose and quietly, but firmly stated, "Brother Owen, I think it would be a good idea if you got back to your text." (I was not present, and Othermama subsequently denied that this actually happened. Nevertheless, it is unlikely that the story was fabricated from thin air. I think no one doubts that one way or the other, Otherpapa conveyed to Reverend Owen the idea that the pulpit of the church should no longer be used as a pro-prohibition platform.)

Otherpapa and Othermama did not go together to the polls that year, as they usually did; I drove Otherpapa, at an early hour, and Othermama went with her own driver, Nick. Repeal won in the state of Texas, and that it failed in Shackelford and Throckmorton counties in no way offended Otherpapa's pride after a summer's campaign. What did disconcert him was the discovery that he and Othermama had voted on the same side of the ballot. The question was phrased in a complex and confusing way, and some believed that it had been so posed by design to mislead advocates of repeal. In this particular instance it had certainly done so. When it first emerged at the dinner table that evening, that both had stamped the left column of the ballot, Otherpapa laughed heartily, and pointing down the table to Othermama said, "You voted for the return of the saloon." Watt, who had been a judge at the election, quickly corrected this misimpression by stating that if, as he had reported, Otherpapa had voted on the left side of the ballot, he had, in fact, actually voted to retain prohibition. Otherpapa never saw the humor of this and no one else dared laugh.

However interested and active Otherpapa always was in all campaigns, he was wary of predicting the outcome. He used to say that there were three things that no one could ever predict with assurance: how an election would go, what a jury would do and whom a woman would marry.

There was another occasion on which Otherpapa stood up in church to admonish the minister, and that was at the time of the dedication of an organ that the family had installed as a memorial to your great-great-grandmother Matthews. Reverend Owen, who was conducting the dedicatory service, was waxing increasingly fulsome in expressing the appreciation of the church and congregation for the generosity of the Matthews family in making the gift. He had, by no means, finished when Otherpapa stood up and terminated the proceeding with, "That will be enough, Brother Owen." Even Othermama never denied that he did this.

IN *INTERWOVEN*, Othermama refers on one occasion to Otherpapa as "a real heartbreaker at eighteen" and again, at the time of their marriage, as her "Prince Charming," but I could never see much evidence that romance or sentiment played a major part in Otherpapa's life. Matter-of-factness was more characteristic of his personality, and he could be as stoic as any Indian in his emotional reactions to whatever circumstances or events.

Otherpapa and Othermama were married, as we have already noted, on Christmas Day, 1876, and to have their wedding anniversary fall at that time always added special significance to the holiday season, especially after 1926, when there was a plenary gathering at Lambshead to celebrate their fiftieth anniversary. Christmas of 1930 found them in Houston with Aunt Sallie and Juddy, and the latter loves to recount an exchange between Othermama and Otherpapa on Christmas morning while seated alone in front of a fire in the living room. Juddy, coming down the stairway into the adjoining entrance hall, heard Othermama ask, "John, do you remember this brooch I am wearing this morning?" to which Otherpapa replied, "I can't say that I do." "Well," continued Othermama, "you gave it to me fifty-four years ago this morning." "Now, if ever," thought Juddy, "Judge Matthews is going to make a sentimental remark." He cocked an ear expectantly toward the door opening into the living room only to hear, "Yes, a mighty cold day."

Funerals were no more likely than weddings to evoke sentimental expression from Otherpapa, and his condolences tended to be of a rather practical nature. He was a faithful attender of funeral services (which he sometimes referred to as "exercises") for family, friends and acquaintances, and he always had a few words of his own straightforward brand of comfort for the bereaved.

My grandfather Burns lived for many years in Albany, and I can still remember hearing him speak with great admiration and fondness of your great-great-grandfather Matthews (Otherpapa's father) who, to judge from everything that I have heard about him, must have been one of the most beloved men who ever lived in West Texas or anywhere else. When my grandfather Burns died, he was buried in Albany, and my father, in talking with Otherpapa after the service, said: "My father certainly thought a lot of your father." "Yes, he did," replied Otherpapa nodding, and adding, "and he thought a lot of me too."

Ungiven to any display of emotion himself, neither was Otherpapa very tolerant of the collapse of self control in others; "Get hold of yourself" was, given the circumstances, likely to be his message. But when Othermama died, he could not hide the depth of his grief.

As the family chart in the back of the Hertzog edition of *Interwoven* shows, Otherpapa had five sisters, and we used to enjoy frequent visits at Lambshead from three of them, Aunts Bettie, Susie and Ella. There were – and are – strong resemblances among the Matthews and Reynolds family members, but few, if any, equal to that between Aunt Susie and Otherpapa. They were about as alike as brother and sister can be without being twins. Once, when Aunt Susie was preparing to return to Fort Worth after a visit at Lambshead, and was instructing her driver, Brown, in the loading of luggage into her car, Otherpapa began to lend some voluntary assistance, taking out and rearranging suitcases that had already been placed as directed by Aunt Susie. This didn't go on long. "Brother," said Aunt Susie with some finality, "thank you for helping, but I know how I want this done and Brown will do it." I think the reason that I recall this with such clarity is that it was the only time I ever heard anyone tell Otherpapa what to do.

OTHERPAPA'S enthusiasm about higher, that is college, education was, to say the least, restrained. His own schooling had been sporadic, as had that of all the young men with whom he grew up. He and they became successful ranchers and responsible figures of society without the benefit of even a high school, much less college, education; in his opinion the generation that followed could well do the same.

This view was reinforced by the accomplishments of his eldest son, Joe, who left Austin College after one year, returned to Albany to enter the cattle business and had achieved outstanding success by the time he was thirty. This proved Otherpapa's thesis, at least to himself, and he tended always to regard time spent in college as largely wasted. It was Othermama's influence that sent the youngest Matthews son, Watt, to Princeton, and which took the family to Austin where daughters Susette, Ethel, Lucile and Sallie attended the University of Texas. None of this did much to change Otherpapa's views, and years later, when I was in my early teens, I can recall Otherpapa being in Norman, the seat of the University of Oklahoma. Observing the students moving about the campus, he commented with undisguised scorn, "Look at them, running around bareheaded and with books under their arms."

Books were unimportant to Otherpapa, as were most other forms of cultural expression. Once, after we had been driving around the ranch most of the day and were heading back toward Lambshead headquarters, I said that there was to be company for supper as Bob Nail (the highly talented writer and originator of the Fandangle, then in Princeton) was bringing a visiting college friend out. Otherpapa's response to this was:

"Needless to say he's a parlor hound." When his own grandson, Joe Blanton, one of the most gifted members of our family, came out to the ranch, following his receipt of a master's degree in architecture from Princeton, Otherpapa greeted him the morning after his arrival with: "Well, Joe, now that you are an architect (Otherpapa always articulated the "ch" in this word, purposefully, I was convinced), I have something I want you to help me with. We need a new chute to pour garbage into the hog pen, and I'm sure you can design it for me." There was no indication that this was meant to be funny, and Joe took the entire thing in good-spirited stride.

Otherpapa's lack of interest in the arts extended to the movies, although he did go from time to time. The first talking film he saw was *Cimarron*, based on the Edna Ferber novel about the opening of the Cherokee Strip of Oklahoma. Some of his grandchildren thought it would interest him and persuaded him to go. Just as Otherpapa and his family party entered the theater, there was, in the film, a knock on a door that prompted Irene Dunne (the actress who played the leading role) to say, "Come in." Otherpapa, standing at the head of the aisle, responded in a strong voice, "I intend to. Have you plenty of room?"

I cannot remember when there was not a phonograph at Lambshead, and I am sure that no machine was ever given more energetic use. Each summer, there were two or three especially popular records among them through the years, the music from such old shows as *"Sunny," "No, No, Nanette," "Dearest Enemy,"* and many others of the same tuneful variety. One summer, the red hot favorite was a song called "He's a Devil in His Own Home Town," and it received a steady daily workout for several weeks. One afternoon, Otherpapa, seated at the corner of the front porch (from which vantage point he could survey whatever might be going on in any part of the "trap" – the fenced area around Lambshead headquarters) called, asking to see the record that was being played. The grandchildren present at the time, delighted that Otherpapa would express an interest, vied with each other to be the one to take the record from the phonograph and go racing to Otherpapa's chair with it. It seems to me that Bill Blanton won. Otherpapa carefully read the label and then, standing up, gave the record a whirl that would be the envy of today's champion Frisbee thrower. With a group of open-mouthed, young observers watching its flight, it shattered into powder against the bluff beyond Lambshead creek.

WHATEVER Otherpapa may have lacked in interest in books and cultural subjects in general was more than compensated by Othermama, who was an ardent reader and student all her life. There was a good library at Lambshead, both current and classic, and that so many of the Matthews grandchildren are avid readers owes some of its attribution to the encouragement they received from Othermama. Given the relatively meager and sporadic schooling of her girlhood, her early marriage, and her responsibilities as the wife of a ranchman and the mother of nine, it is hard for me to figure out how Othermama found the time to make herself the highly cultivated person she was. As I grew up, it seemed to me that she knew everything there was to know about literature, history, mythology, the natural sciences and almost anything else. And she did everything she could to stimulate and encourage interests of others along the same lines. She could have written a handbook on the flora and fauna of West Texas. Even though I later had a college semester's course in astronomy, most of what I now remember about the stars dates back to the indescribably beautiful nights when we would lie on our backs on canvas cots in the front yard of the Lambshead house while Othermama would identify the various constellations and individual stars for us. Where she learned all this I still don't know, but she improved her mind and enriched her life, and the lives of all around her, every day she lived. She delighted in what was at hand instead of yearning for things out of reach.

Otherpapa was little, if any, more interested in sports than the arts and paid scant attention to the American and National League baseball competitions, which, of course, were always in progress during my summers at Lambshead and which were the "golden years" of baseball, with Babe Ruth, Ty Cobb, Tris Speaker and so many others of the all time "greats" of the diamond at their zenith. He was somewhat critical of the Reynoldses for having a polo field on their Kent Ranch, and once refused a high offer for a horse from the Lambshead string when he learned that the prospective buyer intended to train him for polo. Not only did he not care much about sports himself, he was not too keen on his grandchildren devoting time to them. We had a croquet set (if that can be classified as a sport), which was regularly withdrawn following outbreaks of violent arguments, a special feature of croquet, and swimming was encouraged. Horseback riding was a daily activity, of course, but not classified as a sport at Lambshead. In later years, when Othermama and Otherpapa built a house in Albany right next to the golf course, I never heard him make a single favorable reference to the game, but, several that were not so favorable. Strangely enough, I don't recall his ever expressing an opinion about rodeo.

ONE SUMMER, along about July, there was an unusually bad outbreak of screwworms among the cattle and extra men were needed to help doctor them. Otherpapa telephoned Jim Reynolds, Othermama's great-nephew, then about sixteen and an able young cowboy who lived in Albany, and told (not asked) him to be ready to come out the following day for at least two weeks to help with the work. "I'm sorry, Uncle John," said Jim, "but I won't be able to. I'm running a ping-pong parlor." "Ting tong, hell," growled Otherpapa, "you have your saddle and stuff ready to be picked up at nine o'clock tomorrow morning." Jim was on hand with his gear when we drove in the following day; he didn't say what happened to the ping-pong parlor, and certainly Otherpapa didn't ask.

Albany in those days was a good hour's drive from Lambshead, but even so, there was usually one car, often two, going in for church on Sunday mornings. If we did not go to town, Othermama would tell Bible stories to the grandchildren or find another way of devoting at least an hour to some sort of religious observance. She was an authority on the Bible and her faith was as simple, as strong and as natural as a tree. She encouraged all her grandchildren along the same line without ever being puritanical, dogmatic or emotional, and one of the most compelling arguments in behalf of Christianity that I know is that she was such a devout believer. One of her favorite stories about her grandchildren, which she used to tell often, involved my sister, Betty, then about seven, who was invited by Othermama one Sunday afternoon at Lambshead to join her in learning a few verses from the Bible. Betty, who apparently had other ideas in mind, demurred, saying, "I already know all the Bible verses, Othermama." When Othermama exclaimed, "Why that's wonderful, come and let's recite the twenty-third Psalm together," Betty maneuvered a modest retrenchment with, "Well, there may be two or three I don't know."

Two things occurred in 1929 to bring an unalterable change to my summers at Lambshead. One was the death of Sallie Joe Casey, who was my special pal and who is still an integral part of my memories of those summers. She was nearer my age than any of the other grandchildren, and in whatever activity, her companionship added zest. She was good at everything – riding, swimming, any game, music – a keen competitor, but a good loser and a generous winner; she usually won, no matter what the contest. She was a talented mimic and one of her favorite subjects was Otherpapa. There was, as the old saying goes, never a dull moment when Sallie Joe was around; when she left, a sparkle left with her. Lambshead was never again quite the same for me.

That was also the year that Otherpapa and Othermama built their home in Albany, and, therefore, the last summer that they resided at Lambshead. I continued to drive for Otherpapa for two or three years, but it was never the same making the round trip Albany-Lambshead instead of the other way around. It never seemed right to be leaving Lambshead in the late afternoon rather than arriving there at that time.

But, as the much-quoted French saying goes, in translation: "The more things change the more they are the same," and that applies to Lambshead to a marked degree. Even with all the noticeable changes that the years have brought, it is remarkable how essentially the same

LAMBSHEAD IS TODAY as

the place of our childhood summers. There is more mesquite – a lot more – and many more deer. There are fewer jack rabbits, no prairie dogs, but many more turkeys. The Clear Fork is sadly much changed as a stream, but its banks, bottoms and trees are as beautiful and interesting as ever, and the sound of locusts can still be heard all along it with an almost painfully nostalgic echo. The nocturnal coyote chorus is as audible as ever; the sky, both day and night, is as big as ever and the stars are no less glittering than when Othermama used to identify them for us. The breeze at night and in the early morning still has that special sort of muted sigh if you are on a sleeping porch or in a room with an open south window where you can hear it. It makes you want to turn over and go back to sleep; but, not as much as hearing rain on the roof of Lambshead house, which, as I have said, is still one of the pleasantest of all sounds to me.

In the foreword to *Interwoven*, Othermama wrote, "It is possible, if not certain, that our grandchildren will live to see many new discoveries in the sciences, discoveries as wonderful as the radio, if not more so. But with all the new inventions and innovations that may come in their lifetime, it is doubtful if their mode of living and their surroundings in their old age will greatly differ from that of their youth. At least it is unlikely that there will be the great contrast that there is between our life today and that of our early pioneer days." Despite supersonic aircraft, space travel, imminent two-way television, electronic cooking, etc., I believe, as one of the grandchildren approaching, if not already in, old age, that that judgment has been proven correct.

But if the mechanics of living have not changed during the past fifty years to a degree equal to that of the preceding fifty, other elements of life have altered more drastically, with an impact more significant than that made by developments in the fields of communication and transportation. I often ask friends (of my own age) if they know of any place in the world where life is not becoming less agreeable with the years, and I have yet to hear a single nomination. There is no need to enumerate the reasons; most of them are results of the very technological developments that Othermama remarked. For me, Lambshead has changed less than any spot I know, and during my thirty years in the Foreign Service, most of which were spent in distant parts of the world, I never failed, on my trips to the U.S., to "touch base" at Lambshead. I do not mean to project an Antaeus analogy, but the effect has not been dissimilar; I have always left with renewed spirit.

And for me, it is still as it has always been, with the important addition of a patina of memories so clear that they are like part of the living present and so real that they lend to the very place itself an almost animate sense of being, as though there has never been an end to the summers at Lambshead.

Lambshead Sheep